PENGUIN BOO

HERA LINDSAY

'By turns bleakly hilarious and peppered with pitch-perfect similes . . . [*Hera Lindsay* has made me, like many others, more excited about poetry than I have been in a long time'
Lucy Rhiannon Coslett, *Guardian*

'On more than one occasion, while working through a poem, I have found myself asking, "what would Hera Lindsay Bird do?" There should be bumper stickers. Bird's debut, the self-titled *Hera Lindsay Bird* is an exhilarating read, but what most enthrall me are her extravagant and cartoonish images . . . Bird is an enfant terrible'
Lucy Tunstall, *Poetry*

'Much has been made of the sexual nature of her writing, but really, Bird's tendency to feed the reader mildly pornographic images . . . is the least interesting thing about her. Her sexual references are often sly jokes, the punchlines delivering a sharp jolt that opens you up for lovelier lines that lie scattered all around. It's a cunning trick, giving the illusion of reckless intimacy, as if the reader's being dragged into the poet's very bedroom. But really, Bird is nowhere near the bed. She's over at her desk, scribbling furiously, thinking hard, quite possibly laughing to herself. Or maybe she's out in the sitting room, watching sitcom reruns and shouting at her telly . . . Bird bangs vivid images against one another and jump-cuts from the intensely intimate to the casually conversational . . . she is perhaps our own fledgling Frank [O'Hara]: loose and sloppy and spirited and sincere, a gifted show-off who's plugged into the life-giving voltage of pop culture and blessed with a bloody good sense of humour'
Grant Smithies, *Sunday Star Times*

'[Bird] shows a rare, self-effacing self-reflexivity in an age of narcissism . . . this is a poet who is not just using language as a tool, but as an art form . . . The depths of the emotional space in this work – taken to the realms of the ridiculous – are extraordinary to fathom and relish as a reader'
Kelly Malone, *Cordite Poetry Review*

'Even in the most sombre poems, Bird's language is surprising and delightful . . . [She] draws revelation from the mundane . . . there is a satisfying defiance in *Hera Lindsay Bird*, the poet positioning herself against conservatism and authority . . . Her work acknowledges that everything is absurd, the system is fucked, but we – indefatigable – will keep making art and we will do it how we want'
Jessica Alice, *Kill Your Darlings*

'Garrulous . . . impressive . . . Somewhere about halfway during my first reading, I found myself laughing until it hurt'
Airini Beautrais, *Listener*

ABOUT THE AUTHOR

Hera Lindsay Bird has a MA in poetry from Victoria University of Wellington, where she won the 2011 Adam Prize. Her work has been published by *The Toast, The Hairpin, Sport, Hue & Cry, The Spinoff, The New Zealand Listener* and *Best New Zealand Poems.* In 2017 she won the Jessie Mackay Best First Book Award for Poetry and the Sarah Broom Poetry Prize. *Hera Lindsay Bird* is her first collection; a Laureate's Choice poetry pamphlet, selected by Carol Ann Duffy and titled *Pamper Me to Hell & Back,* will be published by smith|doorstop in early 2018. She currently lives in Wellington.

HERA LINDSAY BIRD

Hera Lindsay Bird

PENGUIN BOOKS

PENGUIN CLASSICS

UK | USA | Canada | Ireland | Australia
India | New Zealand | South Africa

Penguin Books is part of the Penguin Random House group of companies
whose addresses can be found at global.penguinrandomhouse.com.

This edition first published in New Zealand by Victoria University Press 2016
First published in Great Britain in Penguin Books 2017

005

Copyright © Hera Lindsay Bird, 2016

Printed and bound in Great Britain by Clays Ltd, Elcograf S.p.A.

ISBN: 978–0–141–98740–8

www.greenpenguin.co.uk

MIX
Paper from
responsible sources
FSC® C018179

Penguin Random House is committed to a
sustainable future for our business, our readers
and our planet. This book is made from Forest
Stewardship Council® certified paper.

CONTENTS

for Angelo

WRITE A BOOK

To be fourteen, and wet yourself extravagantly
At a supermarket checkout
As urine cascades down your black lace stocking
And onto the linoleum
Is to comprehend what it means to be a poet
To stand in the tepid under-halo
Of your own self-making
And want to die....
Far away, in a field of wild orchids
Is a backwards sentimentality
Like a Christmas card with the robins scratched out

Well, it was Oscar Wilde who said sentimentality
is 'the desire to have the luxury of an emotion without paying for it'
Like................when I masturbate and think of nuns
Yet never go to church at Christmas?

Now I have a Masters degree in poetry and no longer wet myself
But I still have to die in antiquated flowers
Does this make me sentimental?
Well, who's to judge
You can get away with anything in a poem
As long as you say *my tits* in it
But it's a false courage to be so..........modestly endowed
And have nothing meaningful to say

You might think this book is ironic
But to me, it is deeply sentimental
like............if you slit your wrists while winking—does that make it a joke?
To be alive
Is the greatest sentimentality there is
And I live to be sentimental
And I love to be alive
Always weeping at the end of a movie
Over the frosted carriages of yesteryear

I wrote this book, and it is sentimental
Because I don't have a right-sized reaction to the world
To write a book is not a right-sized reaction
To put all your bad thoughts on paper
And make someone else pay for them

My friend says it's bad poetry to write a book
And I agree with her
I agree with her......................................in principle
But I wrote a book anyway
And I named it after myself
My name is Hera Lindsay Bird
This book is called Hera Lindsay Bird
I wrote it, and I mean at least 75% of it
And if that's not sentimental

Well..
One day I'm going to have to pay for it

MIRROR TRAPS

I want to lie naked &

                    face down

        in the beige epicentre
of my despair

/

against the   fringed tessellations
    of an inner-city graveyard

tombstones   wilting in the heat

                                    like black candles

I want to lie alone &
    trembling
in my hot   neural vacancy

like a jet shadow

                    across a distant field of corn

emitting
many slow   blinks of the heart

& never have a job

I want to lie each night
                    in the overlapping   heat

    of your absence

        &

                            shuck my heart

into fresh transparencies

    of repentant love

black pheromones pour   out of your eyeholes

mirrors curl   in the sunlight

you smile at me &
      cool beads   float   through my heart

        like the inner   pellets
of a frozen baby rattle

&

                           the overall ache
               of never having touched you

wedged
like a double-sided battle-axe
in the cleft   of an antique rocking chair

          still rocking

with its slow   elliptical

                     murder force

the soft black
                drumroll of your gaze
breaks over me
like a molten wave of   snow
     & my heart

blinks

& flares

          like the yellow gills   of a taxicab

               when you look at me
with your soft austerity

                                        like baby epaulettes

It's bad poetry to have a body
      & want to touch you with it

even worse.........................to be allowed to
           as you stare at me

                    across the silence

of your rare   anti-camouflague

& tell me what it is you have wanted

It's bad poetry to have a body
and a bad life too

                              to get everything you wanted
but still walk away
                          for no other reason

but..........the unspecified wrongness of   your blood

      & all you can do
      is lie face down on the carpet

& wait for the heart to finish   buffering

it's love that plummets you
        back down the elevator shaft

& it's love you go missing to

buying candles from an inner-city megastore

there is something wrong with you

there is something wrong with you that is also wrong with me

I want to lie very still

in a discount facial peel

cucumber slices
floating on my eyelids

like a double-salad monocle

I want to stare   out the window

in a deep   optic hunger

until everything burns

with the mohair of loneliness

& never be touched

I want to lie awake each night

& be struck by
    oscillating waves of

   regret

the heart like a cold sleigh drawn
    again & again

through the dark avenues of spring

        always towards your silence

MONICA

Monica

Monica

Monica

Monica

Monica Geller off popular sitcom F.R.I.E.N.D.S

Is one of the worst characters in the history of television

She makes me want to wash my eyes with hand sanitiser

She makes me want to stand in an abandoned Ukrainian parking lot

And scream her name at a bunch of dead crows

Nobody liked her, except for Chandler

He married her, and that brings me to my second point

What kind of a name for a show was F.R.I.E.N.D.S

When two of them were related

And the rest of them just fucked for ten seasons?

Maybe their fucking was secondary to their friendship

Or they all had enough emotional equilibrium

To be able to maintain a constant state of mutual respect

Despite the fucking

Or conspicuous nonfucking

That was occurring in their lives

But I have to say

It just doesn't seem emotionally realistic

Especially considering that

They were not the most self-aware of people

And to be able to maintain a friendship

Through the various complications of heterosexual monogamy
Is enormously difficult
Especially when you take into consideration
What cunts they all were

I fell in love with a friend once
And we liked to congratulate each other what good friends we were
And how it was great that we could be such good friends, and still fuck
Until we stopped fucking
And then we weren't such good friends anymore

I had a dream the other night
About this friend, and how we were walking
Through sunlight, many years ago
Dragged up from the vaults, like
old military propaganda
You know the kind; young women leaving a factory
Arm in arm, while their fiancées
Are being handsomely shot to death in Prague
And even though this friend doesn't love me anymore
And I don't love them
At least, not in a romantic sense
The memory of what it had been like not to want
To strap concrete blocks to my head
And drown myself in a public fountain rather than spend another day
With them not talking to me
Came back, and I remembered the world

For a moment, as it had been

When we had just met, and love seemed possible

And neither of us resented the other one

And it made me sad

Not just because things ended badly

But more broadly

Because my sadness had less to do with the emotional specifics of that situation

And more to do with the transitory nature of romantic love

Which is becoming relevant to me once again

Because I just met someone new

And this dream reminded me

That, although I believe that there are ways that love can endure

It's just that statistically, or

Based on personal experience

It's unlikely that things are going to go well for long

There is such a narrow window

For happiness in this life

And if the past is anything to go by

Everything is about to go slowly but inevitably wrong

In a non-confrontational but ultimately disappointing way

Monica

Monica

Monica

Monica

Monica Geller from popular sitcom F.R.I.E.N.D.S

Was the favourite character of the Uber driver

Who drove me home the other day
And is the main reason for this poem
Because I remember thinking Monica???
Maybe he doesn't remember who she is
Because when I asked him specifically
Which character he liked best off F.R.I.E.N.D.S
He said 'the woman'
And when I listed their names for him
Phoebe, Rachel and Monica
He said Monica
But he said it with a kind of question mark at the end
Like...............Monica?
Which led me to believe
Either, he was ashamed of liking her
Or he didn't know who he was talking about
And had got her confused with one of the other
Less objectively terrible characters.
I think the driver meant to say Phoebe
Because Phoebe is everyone's favourite
She once stabbed a police officer
She once gave birth to her brother's triplets
She doesn't give a shit what anyone thinks about her
Monica gives a shit what what everyone thinks about her
Monica's parents didn't treat her very well
And that's probably where a lot of her underlying insecurities come from
That have since manifested themselves in controlling
And manipulative behaviour

It's not that I think Monica is unredeemable
I can recognise that her personality has been shaped
By a desire to succeed
And that even when she did succeed, it was never enough
Particularly for her mother, who made her feel like her dreams were stupid
And a waste of time
And that kind of constant belittlement can do terrible things to a person
So maybe, getting really upset when people don't use coasters
Is an understandable, or at least comparatively sane response
To the psychic baggage
Of your parents never having believed in you
Often I look at the world
And I am dumbfounded that anyone can function at all
Given the kinds of violence that
So many people have inherited from the past
But that's still no excuse to throw
A dinner plate at your friends, during a quiet game of Pictionary
And even if that was an isolated incident
And she was able to move on from it
It still doesn't make me want to watch her on TV
I am falling in love and I don't know what to do about it
Throw me in a haunted wheelbarrow and set me on fire
And don't even get me started on Ross

WAYS OF MAKING LOVE

After Bernadette Mayer

Like a metal detector detecting another metal detector.
Like two lonely scholars in the dark clefts of the Cyrillic alphabet.
Like an ancient star slowly getting sucked into a black hole.
So hard we break sports, leaving the conveners of the Olympics
with a generous redundancy package.

You are a denim tree and I'm the world's fastest autumn.
I am the Atlantic Fortress, and you are General Sherman
taking me from behind.
You stride into council chambers, waving a petition to orgasm.

A lip of cloud brushes the roof of the barn.
The pale trees curve around the eye and back into the brain.

It's like watching porn through a kaleidoscope
or a slow wind in a kite factory.
Like dogs trying to do it people-style, but failing due to the inflexibility of
    their anatomical structure.

A cloud of bats float slowly up into your brain rafters.
You roll down my stockings, like the sun peeling ocean from a Soviet globe.

I want you in a seventeenth-century field, tilling the earth like flesh tractors.
In the red shade of a mammoth
in the Natural History Museum.
In the airlock of a space station, my heart shaking like an epileptic star.
Between the plastic sheets of a lobotomy table
because writing poetry about fucking
when you could be fucking
is the last refuge of the stupid.
It's like getting three wishes and wishing for less wishes.
It's like designing a flag the exact same colour as the sky.
It's like crying over spilled milk before it's out of the cow.
It's like breaking into a field at dawn
and euthanising the cow so you can get your crying over and done with
and immediately begin adjusting to your new lactose-free existence.
But love isn't really like killing cattle
no matter what poetry wants us to believe.
The day is a vault the sun has cracked open
money flying everywhere like really expensive leaves
and here I am begging you to come back
as if you were already gone

HAVING SEX IN A FIELD IN 2013

Is the title of this poem, but it's also a true story about being in love
I am in love with you
While one bird feeds another bird right next to me
they throw their shadows into my life
like black sugar

I love to feel this bad because it reminds me of being human
I love this life too
Every day something new happens and I think
so this is the way things are now

I thought that as a stranger put his tongue between my legs
in the first hour of the New Year
and again as I woke
to a field of slow blowing trees
and right now telling you

Friends, I love everything new
even the first days of heartbreak
when everything beautiful is set alight
the glass fur of the cactus
birds on fire with wonder

I have done many things in my life
I have talked to many people

Some of these people have called me very drunk at one in the morning
These people are my best friends
They are like miles of snow to me
When I listen to my voicemail
I can hear one of them saying
Did she just hang up on us

IF YOU ARE AN ANCIENT EGYPTIAN PHARAOH

I am carving dirty hieroglyphics
into the wall of your tomb
If you are a dead French aristocrat
I am the suspicious circumstances
surrounding your death
If you are a shape-shifting wizard
I am the shape you are shifting into
If you are a fast-moving cloud
I am an entire field of deer
looking up
If you are a sceptical cop
I am a haunted fax machine
If you are a catapult
I am the medieval knight
you are catapulting
I fly over the dark fields of my enemies
corkscrewing the dawn
This is what missing you feels like
Without you
I am just the suspicious circumstances
surrounding nothing
Without you I am just
a regular medieval knight
settling ongoing tenancy disputes
and doing other knight-related activities

like dying thousands of years ago
I rise from the grave to lean
like an ancient wind against your house
Your roof a red eyelid
closed against the sky

When I'm not with you I am like
a lonely wrestler with nobody to break chairs on
When you take off your clothes
the whole room darkens to light you
Your nakedness a pale kite

I want to take you to the river that runs behind my house
and show you where the dark water vanishes between the rocks
but I can't
because nothing runs behind my house
not even a lonely commercial highway
I want to stand with you
on the edge of a lonely commercial highway
waiting for the jumper cables
that will restart this engine
and take us somewhere far beyond
the confines of this poem

I need to have a reason
for the aisles of trees we sailed through
and your hand on my knee in reckless disregard

of road safety recommendations
I need to have a reason
for so many nights of watching you recede from me,
like the ass end of a horse
in the credits of a Western
I need to have a reason
for drinking beer in your parents' swimming pool at night
and how you lay face down in the water
like a body in a celestial crime scene
The stars so many knives
in the small of your back

HATE

Some people are meant to be forgiven
and others are meant to be hated forever...........................
....

I don't think it's right to hate people
It's just that I don't care
To wake each day in a snakeskin negligee
and light myself on fire with such ethical behaviours

Once...........................I tried to give hate up
But I was born to feel a great pettiness
To lie face-down in my catholic schoolgirl outfit
and pound the cobblestones of the Royal Albert Hall

Hate is an old fashioned spirituality
To know that pain will take care of itself
It's a lean justice that doesn't serve anyone
Only itself, like a long retired butler

Well I don't like life without a modicum of hate
This was once a righteous indignation
But now...it is a self pleasuring exercise
A literary revenge is the most humiliating of all punishments
To be stretched on the racks of the poetry industrial complex

Hate only hurts the hater, says conventional wisdom
But conventional wisdom's dead and I am still alive
If this hurts, it hurts like self-inflicted ass slaps
Oh tell me I'm a bad girl, with a stunted empathy complex

Some people are meant to hate forever
and other people are meant to have appropriate reactions

Some people believe in forgiveness
and other people believe in....................dwelling on things

Hate is a rare emotion, because nobody dares feel it
Nobody!...at least not by name
Everyone thinks their hate is just wrong behaviour objections
But there are wrong behaviour objections and then there are
...........................wrong behaviour objections

Hate is a white crêpe box, with voluminous spite ruffles
It's a friendly push off a Tuscan cliff
Hate is a private joke, with only one punchline
or a statue in the courtyard with a Bad Attitude

To hate is to glory in bygone hurts
Like an antique canon you never have to load
My hate is a genial hate with 'a modern-vintage aesthetic'
like clocking someone with a non-stick frying pan

As a child, my dance instructor once told me to stop rolling my eyes
I was very petulant, and accustomed to lavish praise
I'm not rolling my eyes, I said, *I'm looking at the ceiling*
And I was...with modern jazz contempt

Hate is an emotional aristocracy fallen on hard times
It's like eating nothing off a solid gold plate
To hate is a cruel vintage festivity
Like a hand-made piñata filled with bees

Hate is a luxurious futility, like a velvet birdbath
Someone wise once said that, and that person was me
And if you don't like it...well
buy me a drink and *you* can finish the poem

Once I tried to understand my enemy
But some people it is less eyerolling not to understand
To hate is a bad behaviour
But I have to feel it anyway
The more they want me less to hate them
The more I smile like a sickle coming down
& they're the bad bad grass

I tell my hate to my girlfriend and she laughs
she laughs and laughs and laughs
she laughs until she cries at the ungenerous things I say
and then looks kind of worried...

CHILDREN ARE THE ORGASM OF THE WORLD

This morning on the bus there was a woman carrying a bag with inspirational sayings and positive affirmations which I was reading because I'm a fan of inspirational sayings and positive affirmations. I also like clothing that gives you advice. What's better than the glittered baseball cap of a stranger telling you what to strive for? It's like living in a world of therapists. The inspirational bag of the woman on the bus said a number of things like 'live in the moment' and 'remember to breathe' but it also said 'children are the orgasm of the world'. Are children the orgasm of the world like orgasms are the orgasms of sex? Are children the orgasm of anything? Children are the orgasm of the world like hovercraft are the orgasm of the future or silence is the orgasm of the telephone, or shit is the orgasm of the lasagne. You could even say sheep are the orgasm of lonely pastures, which are the orgasm of modern farming practices which are the orgasm of the industrial revolution. And then I thought why not? I like comparing things to other things too. Like sometimes when we're having sex and you look like a helicopter in a low-budget movie, disappearing behind a cloud to explode. Or an athlete winning a prestigious sporting tournament at the exact moment he realises his wife has been cheating on him. For the most part, orgasms are the orgasms of the world. Like slam-dunking a glass basketball. Or executing a perfect dive into a swimming pool full of oh my god. Or travelling into the past to forgive yourself and creating a time paradox so complex it forces all of human history to reboot, stranding you naked on some rocky outcrop, looking up at the sunset from a world so new looking up hasn't even been invented yet.

WILD GEESE BY MARY OLIVER
BY HERA LINDSAY BIRD

You do not have to be good
is everything you deserve for taking
relationship advice from a flock of migratory birds.
Even in poetry I forgive you nothing
not even your new empire of grief.
You take off your dress and stand in the river
your body a ghost on loan
from someone else's past.
Tell me about your despair, yours, and I will tell you mine.
Meanwhile in a hospital gown
Meanwhile in a long-dead language
Meanwhile every morning, the stars in tatters on the snow
Meanwhile the library of Alexandria burning in alphabetical order
Meanwhile an asterisk blowing across the screen like tumbleweed
Meanwhile in the lining of the uterine wall
Meanwhile in hyperbole
Meanwhile every day for the rest of our lives
I return here to ask you how to forgive someone
who was never mine to forgive.

You do not have to be good
Being good isn't even the point anymore.
I just don't think it's real
to think of geese and feel so beautiful about yourself

and so far away.

Yesterday my girlfriend and I borrowed a car

and drove down through the valley

where my mother almost starved herself to death thirty years ago

a huge silver wind blowing in from the sea.

What do I care if there is no justice in this world?

Life is hard

and pain is hard

and it's hard for me to write plainly

about the night my girlfriend told me she still loved you

and call it art.

It did not feel like art.

It did not feel like *a hundred miles through the desert repenting.*

It did not feel like a broken wheel backwards into the sea

But it hurt me.

It still hurts me

Even now

The shadow of new leaves trembling the carpet.

Oh Mary

How will we survive ourselves

And will this life ever answer?

I don't know

Panic and awe are the same to me.

I love life

and I hate death

so when you try to describe to me

what it feels like to want to die

I can only look at you
Like you are a slow-burning planet
And I am pouring water through a telescope.

You do not have to be good.
You do not have to be anything.
This is not an anthem for the world.
This life is a hard life and
It crushes people
But it's also weird and full of heat
Crocodiles asleep in their red tent of hunger.
Puzzle pieces blown up the street
On the road outside the house
We sold all our things and moved south for.

It was winter and we were so in love
Sitting on the floor of her grandmother's flat
watching the news roll in
about the woman who had been chained
for seven years in someone's basement
And just got free.
The next morning we packed all our things
and headed south.
As if it were that easy.
As if there were anywhere to arrive
We could ever return from.

BISEXUALITY

'There's such a thing as *too* much sexual freedom....'
Heidegger wrote that and he was bisexual too
always naked on a black leash, scrubbing the telephone
You think *My heart is a shanty town...with fur curtains blowing*

It's like turning your back on God...........but in a risqué halter neck
Like a rocking horse at auction you go to the highest bidder
You want to come home, but your home was destroyed in the war....
And carefully refurbished, with an elegant leopard trim

The men are bad, and the girls.......................are worse bad
Each day you wake up and have to be the wife again
To be a woman to a woman, is a female double-jointedness
Your heart a black salt lick, in an elk-laden pasture

To be bisexual is to be out of office, even to yourself
Like a rare sexual Narnia and no spring in sight
They won't let you out of the closet to get back in again
Deep in the winter coats, a little snow starts falling...

Everyone assumes you want to fuck them.........and they're right
but you're also bad girl, with a kinky....goodbye fetish
Always bursting into tears in the hotel lobby!
Gliding off in a taxi, with a briefcase full of military secrets

It's hard to know what bisexuality means
It just.......comes over you, like an urban sandstorm
When a fish crawls up onto land?—that's bisexuality
It's an ancient sexual amphibiousness

It's like climbing out of a burning building into too much water
Or climbing out of a burning building.......
into a second identical burning building
Why does everything have to be so on fire? you ask yourself
But when you look down, your fretwork is smoking

Not the well of loneliness, more like a water feature
But a tasteful one, with a hidden power supply
You look out over the hills and the rows of red houses
And worst of all, you don't even like softball!!!

THE EX-GIRLFRIENDS ARE BACK
FROM THE WILDERNESS

The ex-girlfriends are back...
emerging once again from the tree shadows...
into the primordial burlesque of autumn
with their low-cut...
reminiscences... and soft, double ironies...
trembling once again into their
opulent...
seasonal migration patterns
a corsage of wilting apologies
tethered to the bust...

The ex-girlfriends are back...with their
hand-beaded inconsistencies...
& various unhappy motives...
dragging their heart like a soft broom through leaves...
and they go on hurting...like the lit windows
of a dollhouse in winter...
with a too-big horse outside...

The ex-girlfriends are back
but in a romantically ambiguous way...

The ex-girlfriends are back and have transcended
the patriarchal limitations of romance...

unlike the new girlfriends...
still handcuffed to monogamy...
slowly writhing...
with their naughty...post-heterosexual fatalism

The ex-girlfriends are back
with their unfounded Soviet aspirations...
and anti-hegemonic arts initiatives...
draped over a piano on the edge of the thicket
playing the lonely upper hand of chopsticks...
in their vague tropical displeasure...

The ex-girlfriends are back...
and the post-girlfriends...
and the 'let's not put a label on this' girlfriends...
all of them at the same time, walking out through
a beaded curtain of water...
like too much Persephone and not enough underworld...
wearing nothing but an Arts degree...
and the soft blowtorch of their eyes....

You can feel their judgements come down upon you
like too-heavy butterflies...
but there's nothing you can do about it!
and worst of all
they don't even want anything...
they're just standing there...performing many

enigmatic life blinks
re-mentioning Deleuze and Guattari
in loneliness and natural lighting
The ex-girlfriends are back
with their sanity pangs
and various life fatigues...
like a stuffed-crocodile exhibit
still begging for death relevance
in the glass case of your heart
But you are the museum director now!
Walking talent on a stiff gold leash
& there's nothing anyone can do about it!

The ex-girlfriends are back
like the liquidation sale of an imported rug megastore
that's been liquidating for centuries...
getting rich off all that...tasselled goodbye money
as they grind your face yet again into
the hand-knotted...
semi-Persian wool blend...of their hearts
begging once more for closure.

The ex-girlfriends are back
with their pre-distressed sadnesses
and their...talent
unlike yourself
who is both undistressed and talent-free!

Yet somehow still above them all
like the grand arbiter of happiness
laughing in your ermine neck ruff
as you push them one by one
down the waxed fuck-off chute
of their bad erotic failures

PLANET OF THE APES

If there is a designated point at which return
becomes of no return, so far is how far

I am always beyond it.
We sit in the rain of your hangover

and I tell you the story about my dead aunt
who spent her sixteenth year digging a giant hole

in the field behind her house and never said why.
Anna I love you.

I love you in the jittering shade of a historic windmill.
I love you standing in the water wearing the river

like an invisible pair of shoes. I love you here
at the beginning of your only life and almost gone

getting high on your porch, light drifting between us
like ghost sequins.

I've always never felt this way about anyone
but the way in which I've never felt about you

is a way of never feeling so new it's somehow old
like a cave painting of a fax machine

or falling asleep in the attic of a spaceship.
You make me want to think of you in a sentence with me in it.

You make me want to find a collapsed mineshaft
I can call your name in while searching for you.

You make me want to tell you what you make me want
but what can I even say to you—riding a desk chair

through the afternoon like a patron saint
of remaindered office furniture.

I don't know what it means
to walk each night into a field alone

and dig, until you are standing in a hole so deep
you cannot be seen above ground.

I don't know what it means to fall asleep on your porch
and wake with the illustrated guide to *Planet of the Apes* open in my hands.

I don't know what it means to wake each morning and love you
and say nothing, as if nothing

were honesty's default, or maybe just a way
for me to avoid the stupid things I need to tell you like

looking at you is like looking at a beautiful person far away
through a telescope that makes you seem the size you almost are

which is something I mean but don't understand
like the new hieroglyphics of songbirds

or how the world in which I'm saying this to you
is already receding

that looking at you is like looking
backwards out the window of a slow-moving helicopter

into the nineteenth-century cornfield of your face
which my historical inaccuracy

has suddenly emptied of birds.
You make my life feel the size of itself.

You make my life a burning craft
on some distant and unintended hillside.

Anna you are the pale green arm
of the Statue of Liberty

reaching up through miles of sand

LOST SCROLLS

After Mark Leidner

Like a passive aggressive gun that fires......nothing instead of bullets
Or Nostradamus predicting the invention of the Capri pant...
Like a primeval tornado collecting nothing but air...

Like accidentally wishing on a satellite and getting women's golf instead of
    happiness...
Like your dad threatening to turn the planet around and keep driving...
Like throwing your wedding bouquet backwards into a discount sporting
    goods store...

Like substituting inspirational quotes for inspirational estimates...
or dawn through a magnifying glass
Like slowly fingering your girlfriend to Bohemian Rhapsody...

It should be like being buried in a denim-lined coffin......
But it's like a rose in an earthquake...

It should be a bouquet of lilacs shackled to your ankle....
But it's black milk pouring out of the fountain...............

It's like freezing containers of vomit to reheat and pour down the toilet...
or animal activists throwing red paint at deer to save time in the long run...

It's like a calculator for hippies where the only button is 'infinity man'...
or drinking Gatorade in your wedding dress
It's like a garden salad thrown into the blades of a helicopter

It's like something that cannot be said but must be said... and in being said
slows the rapid expansion...of the prison-industrial complex...
It's like your family commissioning a shrugging angel headstone...

It should be like tits at dawn...
or a million trees in winter...
But it's like setting the planet on fire...by letting your kite fly too close to the sun

It's like saving millions on camouflage gear by getting North Korea to invest
    in smart-casual trees...

It's like being so committed to living each day as if it were your last, you spend
    each afternoon having a cerebral hemorrhage in a rest home...

Your neighbourhood is involved in a gang war and you are trying to stay
    neutral by wearing white, and your neighbour is stabbing you repeatedly in
    the chest whispering 'White is not a colour, it's a shade...'

It's summer on the Rio Grande and 10,000 bees fly towards you in the shape
    of your father and say....'What do you mean you're quitting baseball?'...

It's like falling in love for the first time for the last time...
or your dead wife returning to you in the body of a convicted paedophile...
It's like wishing on a star so distant the wish isn't granted until you wake up on
   your forty-seventh birthday with cornrows... and a set of chatter rings...

It's like a tornado in a harmonica shop, or a suicide note burned into a cornfield...
It's like using a mnemonic device based on complex chemical structures to
remember your mother's name...

It should be like a film adaptation of the *Home Alone* novelisations...
But it's like writing the word hunger in gravy...

It should be like fucking in a casket...
But it's sunlight falling on castle stones....

It's like punching someone in the face and saying 'just kidding'...
or trying to find your way out a door museum...
It's the black wind through the maples, and the difficulty of getting tenure...

It's like loading a catapult with a catapult and catapulting it into irony...
or a baby singing itself to sleep...
It's like a post-apocalyptic petting zoo, with cages full of old fur coats...

It's like the bonus level on Tekken where you punch a man's face so hard
he becomes the evil version of himself...
but there's no such thing...as punching a man's face so hard
he becomes the evil version of himself...
there's no such thing as the evil version of anything...

It's like a movie where everything started out...fine
and continued to be...fine
until at the end of the movie it turned out everything had been...fine all along

That's what love is like...
It's like firing a gun into a time machine and accidentally hitting Hitler...
It's like masturbating to a documentary on South African mines and
    ejaculating real diamonds...
It's like wanting something so bad you would die to have it...
but you do have it and nobody is asking you to die...

Not the civil war re-enactors loading their muskets in the field behind the
    supermarket parking lot...
Not the man on the bus, with the Ted Bundy biography
Not even the entire American military complex...

Every night you come over and we watch some film...
about people sprinting through the corridors of an abandoned space station...
or
being stabbed to death...in the glittering wetlands of Louisiana...

and every night nobody comes to our house...
and murders us in our sleep...

LOVE COMES BACK

Like your father,
twenty years later with the packet of cigarettes he went out for
Like Monday but this is the nineteenth century
& you're a monied aristocrat with no conception of the working week

Like a haunted board game
pried from the rubble of an archaeological dig site
You roll the dice & bats come flooding out your heart
like molten grappling hooks
your resolve weakening...
like the cord of an antique disco ball...

Love like the recurring decimal of some huge, indivisible number
or a well thrown boomerang
coming to rest in the soft curve of your hand

Love comes back...
like a murderer returning to the scene of the crime...
or not returning...
yet still the crime remains...
like love...
observed or unobserved...
written in blood on the walls of some ancient civilisation
in an idiom so old
we have no contemporary vernacular equivalent

Love like Windows 95
The greatest, most user-friendly Windows of them all
Those four little panes of light
Like the stained glass of an ancient church
vibrating in the sunlit rubble
of the twentieth century

Your face comes floating up in my crystal ball....

The lights come on at the bottom of the ocean
& here we are alone again...

Late November
we ride the black escalator of the mountain
& emerge into the altitude of our last year
The rabbit in the grass gives us something wild to aim for
It twists into spring like a living bell

I have to be here always telling you that
no matter how far I travel beyond you
love will stay tethered
like an evil kite I want to always reel back in
As if we could just turn and wade back
through the ghost of some ancient season
or wake each morning in the heat of a vanished life

Love comes back
from where it's never gone...It was here the whole time
like a genetic anomaly waiting to reveal itself
Like spring at the museum, after centuries of silence
the bronze wings of gladiator helmets trembling in their sockets...
Grecian urns sprouting new leaves...

Love like a hand from the grave
trembling up into the sunlight of the credit sequence
the names of the dead
pouring down the screen
like cool spring rain

THE DAD JOKE IS OVER

sometimes   when a great civilisation is too prosperous for too long
when a great civilisation marked by rapid periods of economic growth
and decline
expands beyond its own conceptual limits
& ventures into the uncharted space beyond what is......funny

sometimes, when there exists too much of a good thing
and
the market is oversaturated with cringing
and
years of puns have blighted the emotional landscape
a great empire can fall
& laughter grow up from the ruins

sometimes there are dad jokes, and they can't take the heat
wandering from set-up to set-up, in their glistening barbecue aprons
their punchlines wither and dissolve, in the shimmering wetlands of
contemporary stand-up
like snowflakes upon the grill, leaving only..........questions
like how many women does it take to change a joke format???
or
knock knock
....

....

....

& nobody answers
but the black wind of fate

The time of the dad joke is over, and things are getting.........al fresco
their punchlines converted into anecdotes, and refurbished with a Tuscan
    feature wall
It's the time of the mother joke & you wake to find a deer carcass in the garden
nothing on the wind..by Elizabeth Arden

Sometimes you wake up   in the cold light of a new era
with the unerring certainty that your life's work is just for.......sham
like........what do you get when you cross a joke and a poem?
or if a punchline falls in the forest, and no one is around to hear it
.....................................is it time to stop telling jokes in the forest?

I like to commit the sympathetic error of meaning all my jokes
but still.........................I do not think that poetry should be saved
it should be like an attic in sunlight, with the bats scrubbed out
like   you can buy this book & then set fire to it...............for free

The time of the mother joke is upon us and you look exactly like Scarlett
    Johansson
you never looked like Scarlett Johansson before but here......in the time of the
    mom joke you do

you walk deeper and deeper into the setup, with your........vague celebrity
impressionism

you can sense a punchline, and it's getting closer...........................

When I was young, my mother couldn't afford brand-name jokes
All we had to laugh at was................the unceasing bitterness of life
Even now, I am compelled to laugh in the face of heartbreak
but when a witticism is made...

The mother joke is here, and the punchline is
....there is no punchline
it's gone beyond the format of a joke, and is in your blood
everything is wrong, but you can't stop laughing
ancient punishments repeating themselves
like nunchucks on a nursery frieze

The mother joke is here, and there is no punchline
this is a poem, not a joke, and the only way out is death
You stare and stare at your vast superfluity of life
it stretches out beyond itself, like too many razors on a kite tail

EVERYTHING IS WRONG

Everything is wrong, I really mean it Isobel
Everything is wrong and love is wrong
I know you believe me
I know you believe me because I know you know it too
This life is changing me already
Running in the empty field behind the salmon hatchery
I think about you
I think about you and the black star of loneliness
Burning me alive
Isobel this life is a lonely life
And Billy Collins is still undressing Emily
Emily who?
She walked out of this life, death streaming
She walked out of this life and left us her silence
Isobel you are my best friend
Because you are teaching me to speak to pain
I thought I was mad at you but I was mad at you
I thought I was mad at you but I was mad at life
and what I couldn't have of it
Oh Emily is gone, we never knew her
She wrote her lines in invisible flames
And now the sun is burning and so are we
And the filing cabinet by the train tracks is burning too
I like to think of you somewhere far ahead
I like to think of you far ahead of me

What I say to you I say to me
I don't care about subtlety
I don't care about forgiveness or God
All I care about is looking at things
And naming them
A rocking horse rocking on the banks of the river
Animals in their soft castles of meat
None of us are getting out of here alive

DAYLIGHT SAVINGS

I was trying to get at something
how the past illuminates the present
still swinging from the heart's rafters
like a chandelier in an ambulance
back before I jettisoned forgiveness
and went over to the dark side
but describing love is a backwards talent
like a bad mental taxidermy
where everything living comes out stuffed
your eyes forever frozen in the headlights of this poem
as I speed closer and closer

All our jokes
like a laugh track at a funeral
all our punchlines unintended
like the time I followed you
for hours in lingerie
up a mountain, in the middle of a fight
to reach the waterfall you said was there
only to arrive at the top and find nothing
but a blue tarpaulin flapping in the breeze
like a plastic Niagara

Or last Christmas, cutting my hair
on the steps of your childhood home

underneath a poster that said
look to the sun and the shadows will fall behind
but I want to talk about return
and how pain can be a place of welcome
how you took off my clothes on a blow-up mattress
a hand-drawn skull & crossbones
shivering on the door

Daylight savings and the clocks burn

Some dark spring hour stolen from a time
I did not know your name

O Anna
Neither our love nor our failures will save us
all our memories
like tin cans on a wedding car
throwing up sparks
like pumping the dog's anal glands
on our first anniversary
or lifting your bedpan
through an inner-city hospital
or back before all of it
when we first fell in love
the heart like a trick candle
on an ancient, moss-dark birthday cake

and you read aloud on the steps each night
from a book on forensic anthropology
maggots like white static
frosting the summer air

Our love a broken scale
always tipping between laughter and grief
all those summers written in stale diamonds
the black years gone, and a green one
rolling away from the stem
as the telescope drains of stars
& you wake up alive again

I feel a lot of hate for people
and want to ride the white horse
of justice forever in your favour
and mine
and not in favour of your enemies
who I must privately belittle
until they vanish into the footnotes
of the shitty things we say about them
but you remind me
the best justice is unthinking
to ride these broken carriages
through the debris of the past
and never look back

O Anna
let us jettison the manky quilts
of our foremothers
still laughing at the reins
and this poem too
like an expensive fur coat
tried on once but never worn
tossed beneath a moving wheel
never once caring
what died to make it

HAVING ALREADY WALKED OUT ON EVERYONE
I EVER SAID I LOVED

I pause for a moment at your door
And consult my fate
This life is more stupid than even I could have hoped for
Every day a search party gets lost in the snow
With no one to dig them out again
I have tried for too long to act in ways that seem reasonable
Yet somehow, this makes me double-unreasonable?
Like flicking someone's bra-strap at a coroner's inquest
The official theme of this poem is
The official theme of all my poems which is
You get in love and then you die!
Oh write it in rhinestones on the lid of my coffin
Some people are too hard to be lived without

Once upon a time I used to feel like............huh
But then I started to feel a little more like...................................uhuh

Once upon a time I used to feel like.................??
But then I started to feel a little more like...................................????????

Having already walked out on everyone I ever said I loved
Things do not bode well for you
But things do also not bode well for me
Every year life gets less and less acceptable

And I feel uncertain of how to proceed in an appropriate fashion
To anticipate heartache is a grim satisfaction
Like tripping down a staircase in a peach negligee
Or an ancient forest with a new corsage of flames
It pleases me to subject myself to such whimsical hurt feelings
But under my main feelings, I have other, worse feelings
Like an auxiliary moat in which black swans are circling
If I ever die young I'm going to do it in style
.....like a Great Gatsby-themed suicide attempt!

Having already walked out on everyone I ever said I loved
I have so little left to say to you
I pause for a moment at your door
My eyes pouring out across the darkness

Oh let us not be little bitches to one another
Life is hard enough as it is
Life is hard enough and fast enough
And there is nothing in this world worth doing
But shaking our heads in awe

A little wind shifts the branches
A bird flies out of the radio and off into silence

I can hardly believe this
I can hardly believe this life
Every time I knock you let me in

KEATS IS DEAD SO FUCK ME FROM BEHIND

Keats is dead, so fuck me from behind
Slowly and with carnal purpose
Some black midwinter afternoon
While all the children are walking home from school
Peel my stockings down with your teeth
Coleridge is dead, and Auden too
Of laughing in an overcoat
Shelley died at sea and his heart wouldn't burn
And Wordsworth......
They never found his body
His widow mad with grief, hammering nails into an empty meadow
Byron, Whitman, our dog crushed by a garage door
Finger me slowly
In the snowscape of your childhood
Our dead floating just below the surface of the earth
Bend me over like a substitute teacher
& pump me full of shivering arrows
O emotional vulnerability
Bosnian folk-song, birds in the chimney
Tell me what you love when you think I'm not listening
Wallace Stevens's mother is calling him in for dinner
But he's not coming, he's dead too, he died sixty years ago
And nobody cared at his funeral
Life is real
And the days burn off like leopard print

Nobody, not even the dead can tell me what to do
Eat my pussy from behind
Bill Manhire's not getting any younger

NEW THINGS

What's the point of saying new things?
I once said to the man
I had just started seeing
When he said there was no point writing about him
Because he was just another mediocre white man
And the Western canon already had that covered

What is there to say about the world that hasn't already been?
More to the point
Who gives a shit?
Three thousand years of standing at the lakeside
Mourning the fall of the Byzantine Empire
I'm as bored of it as anyone
and Shakespeare too
We should all move to the country and fuck each other's brains out

Still, there are better things to be than original
So maybe I can say jazz apothecary
Or ham pantyliner
But it gives me no pleasure
To mean so little
And get so far away with it

What is there to say about love that hasn't already been
Three thousand years of grass and wind

We lay on the banks of the field behind your house
Oh there is nothing to do in this life

The world describes itself again
Black curtains on the windows, pinned up with needles
All across the field, small lights falling
Like snow on a virgin rollercoaster
And trees, I am still crazy
I can barely look at you
I can barely say the words out loud
I could be dead so many years ago

PAIN IMPERATIVES

After Chelsey Minnis

You have to slap yourself in the face with a mohair glove
You have to challenge yourself to a mini-duel

You have to rub your hands on your thighs and think about pain
A little pain comes on, and you get tiresome again

The past is a bad invention that keeps on happening
And it hurts to think about, like an unpaid bill

It's the wind dragging the desert backwards at night
& it burns you, like a little pastel whip

You have to think like this all day in a cucumber facemask
You have to lie very still and wish you were dead

You have to think 'love has radicalised me' & walk around like Helen of Troy
You have to walk around until the ships burn off

It's beautiful to be so self-absorbed
It's like being cursed with looking
You look and look and only see your fate

This is ~ reading the entrails of live animals ~
This is ~ spinning a crystal ball on your index finger ~

To make a small ugliness large is a grandiose mediocrity
It's like the World of Wearable Art

I write this poem like a chastity belt made of bottle caps
Please don't blame me for all the terrible thing I am about to say to you

It's so sad to be in love and not enough of it
It's so sad to been in love and not be still
It's so sad to be with someone so sad
It's so sad to want to

The moral of poetry is too lonely to be written
It's a sad old hygiene, like Cleopatra's hand soap

This is using a jackhammer to bust open a music box
The box cracks and minor notes come drifting out

Poetry should be democratic—that's the modern view
It's like a murder on a train where everyone did it!

This is a shared misery, like crying someone else to sleep
It's the sugared hole at the top of the mountain where the flag goes in

It's a bad crime to say poetry in poetry
It's a bad, adorable crime
Like robbing a bank with a mini-hairdryer

I should never do it—and nor should anyone
But it's boring to be so tasteful.
It's like never masturbating to Lucy Liu

I write this poem like double-leopard print
Like an antique locket filled with pubic hair

You have to stay up each night as a love punishment
You have to handcuff yourself to the past and swallow the key

You have to think tragic sex thoughts like *fucking in a casket*
You have to say true-sounding things and never mean them

You have to look people in the eye, and say 'uh oh'
You have to drag your heart across the room like a heavy chair

You have to tell yourself what you need and do the opposite
You have to be staggered by the cruelty of it

Life!
I should never have thought I could do it
It's like playing the violin in fuzzy handcuffs
It's like the punchline to a long-forgotten joke
Ground down by empires
Blown across millennia by the black winds of destiny

This is breathing through a megaphone
Or begging for mercy in a Russian phrasebook

I write this poem like an obituary in Comic Sans
I write it like suicide hotline hold music

This is a raunchy philosophy, like losing your virginity to Plato
It's like doing a line of sherbet off a toilet seat

This is a teenage sadness, like going to sleep in a prom dress
This is putting on mascara to cry yourself to sleep

You have to make a career out of your pain
You have to pinch yourself and think *ow* like you mean it

You have to live to an old age and regret many things
You have to stay alive long enough to want to

You have to fall in love all over again
With the same person all over again

You have to believe in forgiveness, but never do it
It's an unfair generosity, like having to share a grave

A year goes by and you start having dreams
Wet black flowers pouring out of the telephone

The past stirs behind you on a windless night
It overcomes you like a luxury blow-wave

This is an extravagant poverty—like an IOU in a stripper's g-string
It's like wet sequins blowing down the highway strip

This is a chaste vulgarity, like a well-starched nipple tassel
This is opening your trenchcoat to reveal another
trenchcoat

I throw you down on the bed and kiss your neck
It's a juvenile delinquency, like smashing a toy ukulele

It's like a Ouija board spelling a/s/l?
It's getting me haunted again

This is dull propaganda—like stock footage of the heart
It's like weeping over opera subtitles

This is a well-choreographed melodrama—with a complimentary fainting chair
It gets you smoking in a gold kimono

This is a Pyrrhic victory, like falling in love
It's having so little to say, you hire a skywriter to stay home

This is storming out in the middle of a bar fight, your bonnet strands streaming
You cry and cry, impressing no one

You think you know your life, and then it changes
Time caves in and obliterates the heart

I write this like a sitcom flashback
Like a calendar trembling in a sepia breeze

Someone enters the room and your heart stops
It's an invisible trembling, like a vibrator in an earthquake

This is a higher truth, like a haunted polygraph
It's a church billboard blowing down the interstate

This is sucking dick with a raised pinky finger
It's a bossa nova cover of the Crimean war

This is an upmarket nonconformity, like a Trelise Cooper eco-bag
It's a pentagram in your cappuccino foam

Poetry is a fake nostalgia, like dollhouse curtains flapping in the breeze
It rears up behind you on its antique leg brace

This is like an encore to an empty auditorium
It's a swarm of hornets rising out of the piano

Who was it that said 'the life we enter is not the one we leave'?*
It's an arcane law, like falling in love

It's like a game of musical chairs, but they keep adding more chairs
You get up to leave, but the gramophone goes on and on

*Mary Ruefle

This is a premature ventriloquism
Like a séance for someone who isn't dead yet

This is a fatal pretension—like hanging yourself with a velvet rope
I sign it like a death receipt

This is: stop hitting yourself!
It's pushing a pork roast in a vintage pram

This is an empty cuckoo clock, fast approaching midnight
This is a ransom note with no demands

ACKNOWLEDGEMENTS

Thank you to my family: Vivien, Glenn, Alex, Bex, Sue, Sam and Sylvia. Thank you to Angelo Libeau, Gregory Kan, Andy Connor and Rhydian Thomas. Thank you to Unity Books in Wellington, Especially Tilly Lloyd for her generous support. Thank you to my teachers: Lauren Gould, James Brown, Susan Pearce, Dinah Hawken, Adam Krause, Mandy Hager, Eirlys Hunter and most especially Bernadette Hall. Thank you everyone at Victoria University Press; Fergus, Kirsten, Craig, Holly and my editor, Ashleigh Young. Thank you to Denis and Verna Adam. Thank you to Mark Leidner, Chelsey Minnis, Dorothea Lasky whose poetry made this book possible. Thank you to the publications in which these pieces first appeared: *Hue & Cry, Sport, Minarets, The Spinoff, Left, The Pantograph Punch, Sweet Mammalian,* Cats & Spaghetti Press and Plain Wrap Press.